S0-BBX-573

BACK AND OUT AGAIN

Poems by Mark Morgan Ford

BACK AND OUT AGAIN

Poems by Mark Morgan Ford

Published by:
Cap & Bells Press
New York City, New York

Copyright © 2011 by Cap & Bells Press
All rights reserved. No part of this publication may be reproduced or transmitted in any form or by any means, electronic or mechanical, including photocopying, recording, or by any information storage and retrieval system, without permission in writing from the publisher.

Published by:
Cap & Bells Press
New York City, New York

To Kathy

Acknowledgements

I would like to thank those who helped me polish and publish this collection, including Kieran and Lynne Doherty, Timothy O'Sullivan, Kathryn Fitzgerald and Janet Cohen.

A special thanks goes to my longtime editor Judith Strauss, whose intelligence and patience were greatly tested on these fledgling poems.

Apologies in advance to Mark Ford, the British poet, who will surely object if this collection is mistakenly attributed to him.

And to my three sons, Liam, Patrick and Michael, my wife Kathy, to whom this book is dedicated, and to my friends and family members who inspired these poems.

Table of Contents

Coming Back From the Safari

There we are
Head to head
Mouths open
Eyelids shut
Bumpity
Bumpity
In the back seat
Of Dorsey's
Land Rover
Gabrielle
And Miguel
And Kathy
Sandy too
And that guy
Who picked and
Picked his nose

Bumpity bumpity
In that rickety car
Riding the rutty road
From *en brousse*
Back to our little house
In old N'djamena

(Before the sun rose Pascal woke us, whispering,
"*Patron! Patron! Les camions sont arrivés! C'est
l'heure à partir!*" And so I stumbled out of bed,
looked back at you and there you were in your bra
and panties, legs and belly bare, stretching, as if we
would live forever.)

In the scented darkness
We listened to our comrades
Tell their *histoires* in French
While crickets chirped gladly
In the dew dappled grass
Announcing with fervor
The awakening day
And we knew then that what
We had blithely started
Was quickly unfolding
And that what lay ahead
Was nothing that we feared

When the sun rose everything stopped
While it lit up the savanna
Glittering on the fields of grass
And glowing on the tumbleweed
Ficus trees and jacarandas

For all of that morning through the grasslands
We drove on, looking for little wonders
And found them, one by one, to our delight
And then suddenly we saw the lions
Two prides there were lying in little clumps
In the shade of a leafy canopy
Of acacia, looking so like kittens
Placid, almost meek, they looked up at us
As we eased our truck just up beside them
Rolling down the windows we spoke to them
First with the respect royalty merits
And then, as they ignored us, more boldly
And finally shrieking like hyenas

We got the king to lift its lofty head
And it seemed to me I was his master
Fearless, I opened the door and stepped down
And in one heart stopping moment he rose
Turned toward me and before either of us
Took our next breaths I was back in the car

We roared away, billowing dust
Knowing how all jackals must feel
Alert and in love with life and laughing

An hour later, riding home, we fell
Into some needed sleep, head against head
Dreaming not of lions but miles and miles
Of sun-lit, spiraling-out savanna

And still today when I see this photo
I can remember how the sunlight felt
On my face, half-asleep

Facts to Be Aware Of

1. At minus ninety
Your breath will freeze
In midair
And fall
To the ground
Watch where you step

2. Antarctica is the only continent with no owls
So make provisions when packing to go there

3. All of Forest Gump's still photos
Picture him with closed eyes
Think about why you didn't notice that
Adjust your perspective accordingly

4. There are 2,598,960 possible hands in Texas Hold 'Em
And just as many chances to go wrong in Oklahoma

5. A ten-gallon hat holds three quarts of liquid
Three quarts of liquid is more than
    two quarts of blood

6. In 1941
When Thomas Edison died
Henry Ford captured his last breath
In a bottle
When Henry Ford died
His last breath was too warm
To fall and so ascended

Flora Aphrodite

Named for beauty and for love
You are ugly and loathed
Notorious for eating flies
You feed on ants

Your spiny-edged leaves
Are split like half-truths
Tickled by tiny feet
They clutch and seize their prey

From a bright, unsullied dynasty
Whose name itself is Sundew
You practice your deceit
In shaded swamps and dim-lit bogs

Dionaea muscipula
The scientists call you
But to me you are love's promise
Beautiful, inscrutable, deadly

Fireside Angel, 1937

Galumphing clumsy beast
That tramples, then destroys
Everything in your path

Glad, hoof-footed monster
Dancing, arms triumphant
In a wild-skied wasteland

L'Ange du Foyer ou Le
Triomphe du Surréalisme?

There before you an incandescent light
That begs the unanswerable question
Is it a vision of your bloody war
Or the image of your cloistered artist?

Memory is false but so is feeling
I write thirty poems in thirty days
But can't remember a single line
And yet new lines trickle in like water

CB had his own patois
And wrote and spoke it rudely
This impressed his acolytes
But troubled his detractors

In the morning, at my keyboard,
Like a half tube of toothpaste
I squeeze out another line
Pressing harder every day
To extract a smaller yield

It has been said that the great Bob Dylan
Pilfered many of his best poetic lines
From a poet – I say this is the kind
Of horseshit only a critic could say

I promised that I would come home
Because you bravely asked me to
But when at last I conceded
You were gravely disappointed

Everything you see and hear
Everything you love and fear
Everything you smell and taste
Everything you save and waste

A witch's brew in a cast-iron pot
Spewing fetid fumes and overboiling
Who can say whether the carrot
Went in first or the potato?

What builds the fire?
What makes the stew?
What cooks the broth?
What drinks the brew?

Some, who believe in god,
Feel his juice inspiring
Those less sure of such things
Suspect faulty wiring

Monster angel, happy beast
Shredded rags and devil's feet
Freedoms trampled
Love released
Fear victory, love defeat

Beautiful Suffering

You
Bound
Hooded
Legs folded
Lithe, lotus-like
You bend forward
Hands tethered behind you
The sinewy muscularity of your arms
Your head, shrouded, is resting on your knees
You are exhausted, waiting for what awaits you
Someone is there to take your picture
And put your image in a book
A coffee-table book
Another arrangement
In gray and black
In which you
Are almost
Beautiful
Pretty
You

Ode to a Drinker

When the spirit leaves
Form arises
When the spirit leaves
Form arises
When the spirit leaves
Form arises

So the master said
It should be noted
After fame arrived

After the drinking
After the shouting
After the fucking
And the sorting
After the sweet
Numbing
Pleasure of
Sorting
Was
No
Longer
Needed

Defiant Poser

Nineteen Eleven
Round and doe-eyed
In a linen smock
Flowers beside you
Tick tock Tick tock

Nineteen Twenty-Six
Black on white on gray on black
You sit assured and staring back
As if at eighteen years you knew
The world that would be watching you

Nineteen Twenty-Nine
Newly wed, you sit for us, a camera's dish
Your husband, mammoth like, beside you
Grinning like a boy who's hooked a fish
You are already tired of something – it kills me

Nineteen Thirty
In San Francisco they love you
Your Indian jewelry and ceramic beads
Your braided hair and red barrette
Your eyebrows and your cigarette

Nineteen Thirty-Two
Look at me, please
Smile, please
Please…
Okay, don't
I won't

Nineteen Thirty-Three
In front of a mural, half done
You sit, posed in profile
You are painting yourself
Yet you are already a painting
The maestro looms beside you
Over your pretty shoulder
He is whispering praises
He has the posture of a lover
Who will never leave you

Nineteen Thirty-Four
In his studio in the filtered light
You sit, slumped back, tired again of something
He sits next to you, diverted and upright
A new pet, a monkey, has caught his attention

Nineteen Thirty-Seven
Leaving the cathedral
Wrapped in a shawl
Beside a stone column
Against a wood door
Arms in alabaster
Lips painted black
Your eyes dark
And limpid
Who wouldn't love you?

Nineteen Thirty-Eight
Posing with Don Diego
One hand, sister-like, on his shoulder
The other, palm up, framing the shot
Your bird-fragile slenderness leaning
Against his tousle-haired, denim-clad bulk
A perfect triangle, a perfect shot
There is nothing accidental about you
Nothing that seems quick or casual
That is not also true

Nineteen Thirty-Nine
They say that nobody
Loved you better than Murray
Not Silberstein, not even Bravo
So why are you looking at him that way?

Nineteen Forty
A baby goat in your arms
A framed print of your bedroom flat
Beside the bedside table a phone
Which is puzzling
And on top of that a skeleton
Which is not

Nineteen Forty-One
Your dress is hiked up
Your icons unveiled
A hammer and sickle
The sun, a star
And in your belly
An unborn child
You look wild

Nineteen Forty-Four
At the Picasso exhibit
Dressed like an Indian queen
You are compared to a work of art
The figure of a regal woman
Who cannot match you
There is no chance of it

Nineteen Forty-Eight
Finally, your hair is down
Luxuriant, shimmering, black
It is enough for us, too much
And the sun is in your eyes
Or has the flash gone off?
We want to be there now
With your hair down
We want to ravish you
For love is not enough

Nineteen Fifty
In bed, holding a mirror
Your body armor is a palette
There are bright-colored rings on one hand
And a well-used brush in the other
You are our mentor, our siren
Our sister, our mother

Nineteen Fifty-Two

At the Palace of Fine Arts
Sitting in your wheelchair
You strike one last, defiant pose
The camera cannot help but care for you
Yet in the immensity of the room
With his murals on the walls
You look brittle

Nineteen Fifty-Four

You are lying in your bed
Your eyes as black as darkness
Dress as white as lightness
Your lips are painted red

No more striking poses
No more imposing strokes
You have left us frames of beauty
You have risen to the test
In Don Diego's shadow
You have given us your best

The Shape of Beauty

Venus
Aphrodite
Genius of love
Goddess of beauty
Most brilliant planet
Second to the sun
Shapely statue in
Carved ivory
Or denim
Girl

Learning How to Say Goodbye

Look at the sunrise, you said this morning
I looked up and through the opened louvers
I saw what you had seen and just like that
My heart lifted up from a dark gray sea

Bags in hand, passing little Michael in the living room
I mumbled something
You scolded me, you said go back
I shuffled back. I hugged him. It was fine

And then we did what we have always done
You, walking with me to the waiting car
Kissed goodbye gently at the opened door
Cotton pajamas and a stiff, wool suit

Who can say which flight will be the last one?
Who can say which kiss will be for good?

Just when the airplane lifts off the tarmac
I feel, for a heartbeat, the speed of flight
And touching down again at journey's end
Life's weightlessness, the permanence of loss

My work has been the rush to be ready
But you have always been the break and plow
Our furrows cross and will go on crossing
But they are deep and true and only ours

You and Me Now
(for A.S.)

We are older now
We carry more weight
Your hip is worn out
My thumbs are broken

But we keep moving
Through these high snow banks
That coat warm? you ask
Watch the ice, I say

Forty-one years ago
Our friendship started
A wayward glance, a scuffle
The long forgiveness
Which continues now

The red and the green
The beer and paddles
The conversations
And always the girls

Link to golden link
Poems and parties
Old friends and new ones
Wives, children, time

And yet here we are
On the downward slope
In this bright snowfall
Walking carefully

Patches on a shirt
That hung for years and
Now is worn again
In this sparkling winter

The View This Morning

The sea grapes are now trimmed
Giving us a clear view
The ocean, an old man,
On a park bench, reading
Behind him, on the beach
Early walkers pass by
Looking up at our house
To where we sit gazing
Such the cost of clearing

How to Win Countries
and Influence Prices

Invade a peaceful country
Because you want world peace
Throw a welcome bash
Bring paper hats and pepper spray

If the survivors hate you
Teach appreciation
With cudgels and curfews
Show them you care

Remind them how bad it
Was before you saved them
Show them photos of life
Before you won their hearts

Be brutally sincere
Benignly persistent
Subjects are like children
They need some instruction

Invite each one
To the salvation ball
Provide transportation
Bring gas and lock the doors

Let the world know you
Cannot be defeated
But just in case of snags
Bring party favors and body bags

The First Child

The first child is born well and brave
He must endure the ice and fire
His heart a crucible of gold
A cup to hold his parents' hopes

The second is born slyly smart
For he cannot ever be first
He learns to measure every risk
And weigh his options privately

The last child is born in lightness
He learns to lure what he can't fetch
And feels oppressed by his elders
Yet burns to be equal to them

Still, the firstborn is worst born
He is ahead of everything
And behind nothing except his
Parents' foolish expectations

Dying Goddess

What was he after all?
A wise-cracking bouncer
She was the featured act
The fetching, singing siren
She passed him at the door
And barely looked at him

She was a savage feast
Wild hair, puma black eyes
Cherry mouth, lizard tongue
He loved her tongue and teeth
Wrote bad lines about them
Flesh like fresh apple skin
That sort of boyish thing

But the colors were right
Whipped cream, blackcurrant sauce
Milk chocolate and brandy
Calorie rich, piled high
He should have suspected
There was too much of her
When she sang the room blazed
And the boys burned, leaving
And left at two, smoldering
Nobody, young or old,
Could ever refuse her

After, at the Greek diner,
They ate eggs and bacon
Pancakes and black coffee
She was happy and talked
And talked and he listened
Her teeth and tongue moving

In the early mornings
Driving to Queens College
She rattled on about Poe
And chemistry and math
He made offhand remarks
That unsettled her calm
She said he drove badly

One summer afternoon
They drove to the ocean
And lay down on the beach
Head to toe, skin to skin
In her infinite blanket
Her body, speckled sand
Was a shifting dune
When the gulls came at night
She played a song for him
For him and no one else
It was almost perfect

But there was still something
Missing he thought, yes he
Was almost sure of it
There was something not there

Entering a bar room
Her hanging on his arm
Was like walking into
A church with flaming hair
Every head craned to look
He could hear the hearts stop
Just for a moment and
Then go back to beating
In that she was perfect, he knew
And she knew it also
And that was the problem

Dreaming, she was a siren
And he was a sailor
He could not clear the shoals
The boat screeched, groaned
And settled in the darkness

The next day he told her
"I know what is missing."
"Don't forget the exit."
"You have no soul," he said."
"Damn," she said. "You missed it."

Years later at a party
People from the old days
Noisy and good natured
He saw her on the stairs
In a blood-red ball gown
Her hair black and alive
Her shoulders white and bare
The noise dropped to a hush

It was the best entrance
Of her career he thought
And he was proud of her

But sadness had come
With her, some subtle sign
Of time's unwinding coil
Everyone around her
Giddy, little planets
Seemed somehow unaware
That she was not singing

In a Copse of Hardwood Green

In a dark copse of hardwood green
Two old and gnarled ficus trees
Lift up close to one another
Their rugged trunks nearly touching
As if to form one bulky thing
Their roots, pinioned feet enfolded
Branches, forlorn and leafless gray,
Entwined from decades of reaching
But also in this deadwood gloom
A leaflet uncurling outward
Startling as a heartbeat in stone
That has stopped and then beats again

He Searches for Samantha Chang and Her Pastel-Polyester Cardigan

At 30, she recounts her life, starting at 19
And loving her name, he is happy to listen
And hears about the lava lamps and
Beyond-creepy laundry room and
Her job selling old clothes at a hip boutique
Wearing a "pastel-polyester cardigan,"
Too-much eyeliner, mauve lipstick
And a "beauty-school shag with
The platinum skunk stripe"

A brilliant start, he feels, he's all hers now
She talks breezily about old boyfriends
Dreadlocks, odd jobs and blue-tinged skin
The grimy basements and beer-drinking rock shows
Even country-road car rides with bad boys
And "pot-infused sex" in a "patchouli-scented" apartment

He imagines her house – a lime green cottage
In Key West surrounded by mango trees and date palms
From which she provides oriental massage
And writes tankas on the porch with the parrots

At 21, she tells him, she graduated from beer to vodka
And then from pot to powder at parties
In the morning it was different too, with cigarettes
And wannabe men in well-cut suits with jobs
On Wall Street or Madison Avenue – that too
He is sad to hear this but soldiers on
Hoping that some spark of the pastel perkiness
And deep-rooted Asian kindling might reignite

But the very words she chooses – wannabe men –
And the credentials she mentions are dubious

Now, she says, she is the mother of twins
In "salt-stained clogs" and T-shirts that
    "smell of apple juice"
She lives in an "Upper West Side apartment"
Paid for by her very own "high-income husband"

And now he feels the weight of his hope
That felt like ether just moments earlier
Fall from the zenith of his best intentions
To the pit of his bare and hungry belly
And it lands with a deadening crash

So you see, she doesn't say she's done and had it all
In fact, when she sees a young girl gliding down the street
These days it makes her smile to know that she was once
That young and now writes stories about young girls
"And a China I never knew"

He wants to lecture her: This is not a great story
But an encomium of your former self,
A tapestry woven in self wonder
Without a stitch of irony – precious
Post precocious and a betrayal of your ancestry

And yet he cannot write her off
The beauty school shag and platinum skunk
Still grip him and there is something else
What is it? It's her name – Chang
It's the promise of black hair and eyes

And some magic that will come from that
So he Googles her name
And finds loads of stuff – articles, awards
Citations, an ivy-league pedigree
The *au courant* and *de rigueur* Chinese-American
Immigrant family – impressive and impeccable

Interviewed by some rival, middle-aged author
Who slobbers limp questions at her and lathers praise
She is sublimely unconscious or pitch-perfectly coy
The literary Lolita of his unctuous pandering

That does not help except to excite some envy
The kindling hope, the crackling fire of admiration
All fueled by the combustible name
What is left but to lift the veil and see the face?

He looks for photos and finds but one – but one
That cannot be – and yet it is, the head and shoulders
Of a tall and awkward Jewish girl
Who, he realizes, is named Samantha
And whose high-income husband is a Mr. Chang

Five Death Poems, Tanka Form

#1: For Rand Sutherland
In our universe
Beaming brightest in the void
He held the center
And kept us by jocund tugs
In some close constellation

#2: For Michael Puma
Child of violence
Father to laughter and ire
Brother to kindness
Friend of intemperate foes
We are bearing you with us

#3: For Joel Nadel
Tempest and Torrent
Nothing could stand in your way
To some abhorrent
Except those lifted by your force
And thus carried by your sway

#4: For Joan Ford
You braved all the storms
You never anchored leeward
When calm seas returned
Your ship was taking water
I came too late to save you

#5: For Frank Ford
Ozymandius
Dreamer in Latin and Greek
Mathematician
Teacher, playwright, scholar, geek
Rejoice in what you gave us

There Are Rivers in the Sky

Miles and miles above our living
Beyond the clouds that we can see
Over the clamoring cities
And the groaning, age-old forests
They're running, rivers in the sky

We have robbed our neighbors, murdered
Our friends and sold, for a fool's price,
Every seed we ever planted
We've brought on plagues and pestilence
And a host of calamities
For which we have no names or cures

And yet the rivers flow and flow
Wide, wet rivers, running always
Giving back what we have taken
Giving back what we have thrown away
Penny for penny, dime for dime
Unasked, unseen, unrewarded

In the Morning at His Son's Home

In the shade of the garden gazebo
Beside the fish pond and the Jacuzzi
He sits stooped over the crossword puzzle
Sipping coffee and conjuring answers

Last and strongest drinker to bed each night
First and most buoyant to rise each dawn
He breaks through the morning's conundrums
Like a grizzled sailor shucking oysters

And though the prior night's conversation
Took its normal, familial pattern
From bemused to barbed to belligerent
There is nothing simmering inside him now
Just a bright willfulness to start again

He has done it all – charmed the women
Bewitched the men, killed his wife with charm
And conquered all his children but me
And that irks him when he lies down to sleep

And so he will renew his last campaign
With good humor and wit, intelligence
And all his fox-like charm coiled up to snare
Me, his last, truculent outlying son

At eighty he is much too old for this
But he has made a chain of charisma
A bracelet of sometimes reluctant love
That has all the links completed but one

Looking Down Bowery Street

He feels like an Edward Hopper painting
Writing inside a darkened hotel room
Looking up through a red curtained window
Paused in mid-sentence while outside a cold
Rain-specked April day breaks in the city

From the mirror he sees himself sideways
A man in white underwear and black socks
At a table in front of a window
In a second-floor room of a sad hotel
Hunched forward, looking down Bowery Street

Outside across the road on the pavement
Two men in overcoats sipping coffee
Reading newspapers in a yellow glow
Projected from the restaurant inside

Beside them, in the shade of a doorwell
A waiter huddles, hugging himself, head
Bent up and across the street at a red
Curtained window: a dark figure writing

Please Note: When I'm Gone

Who will care for my library?
Forty years old and aging still
Who will dust the jacket covers?
Or brush a hand across the spines?

Who will vow to read Proust again?
Study Crane's Italian grammar?
Browse Finnegan's book on sculpture
Or pine again for *Lolita*?

Who will study all the spaces?
Not keeping count but keeping up
Tattered gems from dollar boxes
And first editions in wrappers

What will happen when I'm buried?
Will someone come and sort through them
And, stopping here and there to think,
Find a foster parent for each?

Or will they be kept together
And carted off and rudely stacked
In some neglected attic space
With other forgotten pleasures?

What I Know of Ovid

To be born, Ovid said, is to desist
From being what we were before.
And so to live, he did insist,
Is just to play some other score.

And every good we do create
Or grow or shape or reinvent
Other souls must perpetuate
An endless spiral, upward bent

And every evil we design
Is likewise borne in later lives
To fester, grow and intertwine
With other mean or brutish drives

To be reborn is something more
Than falling from a vacant sky
The imprint of what was drawn before
Is etched too deeply to deny

Each life is given choices still
As passions rise more steeply
We pick which grooves we will not fill
And which we'll cut more deeply

Patient Gecko

Patiently sitting
In the unforgiving sun
His chest lifting
He has been there since sunrise
Why is he waiting?

Early Frost

Land too soon frosted
Swallows gone without a song
I am not ready

When Michael Is Gone

When Michael is gone
Who will tend to his bonsai?
Who will water it?
Or trim its tiny branches?
Or celebrate its blooming?

From the Edge of the Horizon Series

1. Along Via Cordona

He walks the narrow Via Cordona
Passing the age-weary shops and thinking
Of a time when life had a clear purpose
When nothing was accidental or lame
When promises made or implied were kept
Or if broken, were fixed by gold or blood
Between the street and sidewalk a row
Of lime trees stands, their roots dusted in soot
Their trunks, ages old, bare-knuckled and bruised
And twisted arthritically their branches
Still bear fruit – small green limes that he can smell

He thinks of Greta and how she was then
When her neck and shoulders were smooth and brown
How her body smelled like sweat and apples
When everything was opened to him
He remembers how the candles flickered
When he let out the shutters to the moon

Against that very door they had fucked
Pressing against her, holding her hands up
Her skirt pulled up against his belly
His underpants pushed down to his knees
When they shuddered she smelled like apples

The last time he had her was in the dark
The candles were gone. She could buy no more
He didn't mind. He took his time, fumbling

She helped him find her, laughing in his ear
And when he left he closed the door gently

2. In the Morning by the Harbor

He goes evenings after working
Walks beyond the old customs house
Toward the docks that are vacant
Where he sips his cup of noisette

It is a very old cafe
Built beside a Roman wall
Whose two stone towers stand still
Ignoring the unprotected bay

He selects his favorite spot
The small table in the corner
By the room's one unclosed window
A safe view of the sunny bay

Alessandra brings him his coffee
He stirs it slowly, takes a sip
Then lights up a Toscanelli
And looks out toward the harbor

Perched on a post in the water
A sea gull seems to glare at him
He glares back in defiance, it's no use
The old bird will not shift its gaze

So he looks away toward the
Piazza Santa Maria

And admires the funiculars
Climbing up the city's hills

And he can almost feel his soul
Being carried up
Above the heavy gravity
Recurrent thoughts on feathered wings

He holds that thought and then looks back
And is surprised to see that the gull
Is still perched there looking at him
He snuffs out his cigar and leaves

3. Spino at the Old Pie House

This is – as you can well see – an old house
It was built before you or I were born
Constructed of that old Florida pine
With a flat, tin roof and louvered windows
Surrounded by scrub oak and palmetto

Come inside – it's just as it was back then
The paneled walls, the stone floor – everything
Bleached with this crust of old sea salt
Check out the zinc counter top and wood-fired stove
Sit here – you can still feel its amber warmth
Now listen – can you still hear the music?
The crackling sound from the record player?
It's the *Tango Della Capinere*,
Still played the way we liked to play it then

If you want to know what it was like then
Look at the table by the one window
Imagine Spino sitting there drinking coffee
For that's where he sat, every morning
Reading the *Gazzetta Ufficiale*
Sketching customers on his notepad
Waiting for his ham and chickpea pie

We kept that table on reserve for him
We were honored that he favored our inn
And so when he failed to come in one day
We were more than a little bit concerned
There were rumors, but we dismissed them all
He was to us a kind and gentle man
Nothing like what was said about him later
Look at that old photo on the back wall
Do you see him in the background there?
At his table, looking up and smiling?
That was the very Spino we knew then!

4. Many Years Later at the Louisiana

The Louisiana was the Tropical then
And it was festive, with a band and sailors
Mambos and salsas and girls brightly dressed
Glittery things to distract us from the
Droning monotony of the terrible war
But that, you see, was more than twenty years ago
Today the stage is gone and there are tables
On the dance floor and the music is recorded

He came every day just before dusk
As imperceptible as a shadow
And sat alone at the corner table
Sipping Pernod and smoking French cigarettes

Harpo played the piano in those days
He played badly but loudly enough
He and Spino knew each other
From the old days but never once
Did I see them even give a nod

Perhaps there was no point in it
What could they say to change the past?
But in Harpo's pocket he kept a photo
He and Spino and Sally on the bandstand
Playing mambos through the bloody war

One day in the future, Harpo thought
He and Spino would finally sit down
And say what had to be said and hadn't

Four Tankas

1. Watering the Willow Branch
Prim in a red vase
A willow branch is standing
Its airy whiteness
Will turn brittle by morning
Yet she will give it water

2. Waiting for Sunrise
Spring cold lifting
Stars chased from the snowy sky
I sit on my porch
Shivering, thinking of you
Waiting for the sun to rise

3. Looking at the Grass
Damp morning coolness
She studies the dimpled lawn
Dew beads on the grass
Too soon the sun will rise up
And smooth every bubbled blade

4. The Farmer's Lament
They took my barn down
And set fire to the pastures
Looking westward now
Over the smoldering land
He can see the moon's white face

Running in the Sand

Running along the moonlit shore
A phantom flickers at my side
Ushered in through the night's portal
A half forgotten memory
Or some cunning, failing dream
I cannot help but look to her
And in that moment she is gone

I have read books about music
That show its impact on the brain
Each note has its proper impulse
Each beat its message to convey
Everything mystical is known
Now or will be before I go

I shudder and set out again
And the moonlight through smoky clouds
Casts purple shadows on the shore
And again she is beside me
Her vaporous breaths in sync with mine
What can I do but keep running?

From the distant plum-dark mountains
A light wind comes, eerily cool,
Like the feathers of an angel
It brushes by me and is gone

And as it passes it whispers:
You are loved
Don't worry
You are loved
I am here
I will stay

The New Writer and Wodehouse

A Formica shelf wedged into a niche
Built under a second-story window
It's not the sort of desk that would inspire
A new writer or his hoped-for readers
Climbing up the spiral staircase he goes
Clutching his precious laptop like silver

Work, memory, the want to remember
How it all persists is the miracle
The thighs ache, the knees pinch, the head hunches
How much longer can I do this, he thinks

Inside, his dead lion, paws outspread, looks
Up with yellow-glass eyes to greet him
He steps over his friend, sits down and writes

P.G. Woodhouse wrote in a tidy room
Full of curious things – a crystal dish,
An old canister, stacks of fresh paper
A walking cane, some cigarette cartons

His typewriter sat on a leather pad
As if everything was in good order
It's odd, he said, how a plot will get lost
As you follow along just behind it

But when you have the line of one in hand
You can hold on to it if you're careful
Like the old man, letting it out slowly
And then working it back in inch by inch

When you've got hold of a plot you play with it
Letting the words roll out tugging
On them – that's what causes all the bleeding

When it is done there is nothing left to do
But worry about the next one, he said
"I don't want to be like George Bernard Shaw,"
     he'd once said
"He turned out some awfully bad stuff later.
He knew it was bad but he couldn't stop."

How to Make Love Thoughtfully
(After White Noise)

What do you want to do?
Whatever you want
I want what's best for you
What's best for me is to please you
What pleases me is to make you happy
What makes me happy is doing what you want
I want to do whatever you want
I want what's best for you…
I'm serious, Sugar Plum
Me too, Honey Bunny

So what do you want, really?
I really want to do whatever you want!
But I told you what that is.
And what is it, Sweetie Pie?
To please you, Cupcake.
Well you can please me if…
If what, Coochie Coo?
If you agree to…
To what, Cuddly Poo?
To do….
Yes?
To do…
To do?
What you want!

Cripes! I told you what I want!
No, you didn't… you didn't tell me.
I said I want to please you
And I said whatever pleases you pleases me.

I understand that, but…
But what?
But I just want to do whatever is best for you…
And I told you – what's best for me is to please you
And what pleases me is to make you happy
What makes me happy is doing what you want to do
I want to do whatever you want
I want what's best for you…

What was that noise?
Someone coming up the stairs!
They're back! Get dressed!
We never have enough time!

What's Wrong With Saran Wrap?

Or Bic pens and lighters?
Camouflage jackets,
Or chicken-fried steak,
Kleenex, Pop-Tarts,
Or Bowflex machines?
Can you say one bad thing – truly
Against the George Foreman grill?

Sing me a song for Keds, can't you?
And for Goodyear tires
Or chili cheese dogs
Or Gatorade or Arrow shirts
Revlon rouge for redheads
And panty hose!

I've had all I can take
Of Don DeLillo
And Joan Didion
And organic greens.
Of tidy little cars
And green corporations
And smart-ass essays by
Feckless fucks
Who tout dreary novels
By navel picking writers
Or praise bullshit art
By dreary egoists
The flouted flatulence
Of bloated poseurs and pedants

I'm going back to the white noise
The granularity of a tubular TV
The sour smell of an old bar
The cold, cheap beer and sharp corners
Where anything can actually happen
Really happen – fast and hard
Where you are done before you know it

Get me out of the smart set
And back to the straight stuff
The blunt notions
And brute gestures
The clumsy steps
And harsh sentences
All that bad language
That harsh, unkempt language!

And fuck everyone who doesn't agree
The critics with their doctrines
The scanners with their timers
Democrats with their pompous dictums
Republicans with their secret hypocrisies
Professors with their masturbatory orations
Every stupid punk and loudmouth brat
Who recoils and shuns and disagrees
Fuck you all and leave me alone
Stay in your world
I'll take back mine

Arlington National Cemetery
Section 60

The grass is new, the headstones bright
Each cut cleanly to fit the rules
Here your choices are limited
Your name, your rank, your date of death
A simple phrase – among a few
Selected to note your service
Not a word that might distinguish
You from the thousands there with you
No hint of what went through your mind
Or passed through your lips at the end
Your lover's name, your favorite shoes
The jolt you felt when your mother's
Slap sent you tumbling, stupefied
Forever wanting to go back
Not the crisp, white cotton jacket
You wore at your first communion
Nor kissing naked Annabelle
On the landing of her staircase
Not the burn of salt in your eyes
When you first felt the ocean spray
Lost among thousands at Jones Beach
Nor those football games with the twins
Nor Mrs. Siemens' approval
The way Sue wouldn't let you go
When you wanted to go away

None of that can be noted here
There is neither the space for it
Nor the stated regulation

For your beliefs if you have them
You can only choose a symbol
Everything else is determined
Just as it has been since you first
Decided to be solider
The food you ate, the clothes you wore
The hard cots you learned to sleep in
Your gun, its bullets, their targets
Everything was taken care of,
Adjured with the proper dignity
By men who had died before you
Everything, including your death
And all its grim requirements

Into This Tranquil Place

Into this tranquil place
This clearing by the stream
Something terrible comes
The wind stirs up the leaves

Now the birds go silent
Now the sky goes gray
And from the west it comes
A roiling wall of black

Now the cracking thunder
Now the torrents of rain
Now the flash of lightning
She hides inside her coat

Overwhelmed, Unprepared
She has no place to go
No plan for an exit
Only herself to blame

Bad News

Bad news isn't mannerly
It doesn't announce itself
It prefers to come to you
When you least expect it to

Bad news isn't courteous
It doesn't beg your pardon
It insinuates itself
Without consideration

Bad news is a good hunter
It sniffs out your weaknesses
Aims its malevolent force
Where you are vulnerable

Bad news isn't chivalric
When it has you defenseless
It won't return your cutlass
But moves forward to the kill

Apocrypha

Who knew their names?
Not Father Brown
Who invited me into the sacristy
To ask me about masturbation
Nor Sister Christophene
Who clapped our ears till they were pink
Not my own mother
Who never lost her faith
Even after eight children
And illness and penury
Had wrecked her body

Dismas and Gestas
Nobody I knew knew them
If they lived they lived only
In the Gospel of Nicodemus
One of many Christian books
We have never read and will not
Without knowing our poverty
Without accepting the truth
That our deaths will be endless

Should You Die Before Me

You told me once should you die before me
I should not grieve your death too long but keep
Your ashes in an urn on the mantel
For one year and then set free whatever
Dust or heartache was left – as if I could
After fifty years of loving you so
Bear the lack of you or stem the fast tears
That would against my will arrive when in
Some distracted, wandering reverie
Your name was called out and turning round to see
Your face found I was again mistaken
And that the lovely woman I loved so well
Had been so meanly ripped away from me
A loss so deep I could not tell its truth
Or from this living death be wakened

Internal Rhymes: Number Two

His thinking dims, he falls asleep
And wakes unsure of where he is
Or what is next or what has passed
There is only this, he decides
And from the brink he starts and stands
And feeling light and heavy too
He pulls the ratty curtains closed
And falls asleep but wakes again
Into fragmented memories
Of a self-assembled nightmare
Built painstakingly over time
All the old friends are long gone now
Broken off the stone one by one
By careless truths and quick gestures
Averted glances and mumbles
Links broken, lines cut, love scattered
Like frightened pigeons from gunshot
Scattering into a clear sky

Internal Rhymes: Number Three

He rises, weary, wishing he could sprout
Feathered wings and fly above the city
But tethered to the earth by gloomy thoughts,
He walks to the window and opens it
And leans out into the raucous city
The weathered grit of progress, the sharp din
The girth of swollen human enterprise
The innumerable, clamoring souls
He breathes it all in and it feels like hope
Exhales, shuts the window and goes to bed

Internal Rhymes: Number Four

He wakes into a morning fresh and clear
And for a moment breathes in hope
Then eases out of bed and showers
And shaves and combs his hair
And dresses carefully
The shirt buttoned
The belt cinched
Shoelaces knotted exactly so
The confidence given
By a life of ease and forward motion
He feints and fakes and dodges dread
Running down the empty stairs
Through the dim-lit lobby
Into the bright, chaotic city streets

Internal Rhymes: Number Five

And what wild and florid bards of chaos
Hail him, the screaming girls, the flower stalls
The hawking vendors, barking dogs in yards
And lots of rubbish, black men playing cards
Squawking boom boxes, shouting at the boys

The gleaming signs of madness and decay
Erupt like goose bumps on the city's skin
Lamps for Sale, Salsa Lessons Two for One
Last week's shopping guides, open windows
Bits of marble, guns rigged from pipes and clay
Shards of glass, garbled promises from whores

And the teeming, raucous total of it
The broken playthings and feckless lawyers
Crack-addled lovers, bond brokers, fag priests
Shredded notes, acne creams and fractured scales
Flat tires, old wars, spoken curses, written lies
Where is the temple? Who is Edwin Meese?
Where can a man find a moment's peace?

Internal Rhymes: Number Six

While in the kitchen Mozart plays
Saki scrapes the pots and pans
Dreaming of another place
Far from the bacon fried in grease
The daily grind of coffee beans
The booths and stools and hopeless fools
The bums and sinners that she serves
The edgy pimps, the nodding whores
As joyous Amadeus soars

Internal Rhymes: Number Seven

He shuts the door and goes to sit
Between a sailor and a tart
And with his elbows claims a space
That's his alone
His eyes are down, his body set
He will not move or make a sound
But takes in Mozart tone by tone
In pulsing movements in his head
Puncturing the thick palimpsest
Of doubt on pain on hurt on dread
And beat by beat a worming thread
Of hope is cut
Where death resided held by hate
Wondering why amidst the noise
And anguished fury all about
This one place would be serene
A sun-bleached isle in a dark storm

Internal Rhymes: Number Nine

He thinks that given any luck
He could find consolation here
Enough to jumpstart his dead mind
To power up his unswitched heart
A moment's calm to drive out fear
The soothing balm
That ordered music brings
When from cacophony's shrieking
Earth's beating heart is detected
New peace is found that first arrives
And leaves as quickly as a chime
Ephemeral as a good thought
Or the impulse to start again

Internal Rhymes: Number Ten

He sips his coffee, has a thought
To begin each morning like this
An hour with her in this exotic place
Time enough to fill a soul's tank
With hope and keep regret away
He lifts his head and studies her
The way she moves, the care she takes
The smallness of every gesture
Even her fingers, her fingers
Which are too lovely to ignore
The way, when listening, she looks off
And yet hears every nuanced word
As if each conversation brings
With it some residual grief
Or, when the music stops, she seems
Robbed of something unnamable
As if some thief in passing stole
Her wings and then restored them
The heart drops, the soul departs
And for a moment everything
Stops and then the heart beats again

Internal Rhymes: Number Sixteen

And so each morning he ventured out
From his dim room to her sanctuary
Passing insensate through the changing signs
That had, in his past, yielded bits of joy
And lifted him a bit from the sameness
That is a rooted part of each ranging day
That pummels us down and flattens us out
Till at some unknown future point in time
Like a gambler at the end of his run
We trade what residue of hope we've kept
For the glad payout of unconscious sleep

How to Remove a Stain

Timely treatment is essential
Attacking the stain when it's fresh
Gives the best chance of succeeding
Allow it to settle too long
And it may become permanent

But the wrong remedy could result
In irreparable damage
So be quick but also cautious
Test each one discretely

Finding a solution that works
Move forward with confidence
Work from the back side going out
You can't be too careful with stains

If the stain becomes permanent
You can camouflage the fabric
Putting blotches here, dashes there
A happy pattern of color
Old fabrics are lovely that way

Sunday Morning
Memorial Day, 2007

Between the head of one marble stone
And the foot of another there is room
Room enough to insert new lavender
In the old vase and a quilted blanket –
The one they slept on – and her blue jacket

She stretches out, face down, head to the stone
Chin propped on fists, legs crossed, toes touching
The smell of lavender in her red hair
She looks around to check on the others
Families visiting other graves

No one is watching her now so she smiles
For what she will do is embarrassing
She clears her throat and talks in her bright voice
Telling what little stories she has brought
The dog's new red collar, Grady's new car
Everything that has happened since Sunday

And then the silence, the aching silence
That makes a mockery of her mute hope
But it is a ritual that sustains her
Remembering anew, she has become good at that
Going through the days, waiting for Sunday
On the bus, leaning against the window
Staring out at nothing, thinking of him

Waiting for Sunday – lying down again
The soft wool blanket in the rough cut grass

Her weight on top of him now, chest to chest
Touching, belly to belly, thigh to thigh
Talking to him about the time between

Kieran: Early in the Process

We meet at the Green Owl cafe
And have our black coffee and eggs
Talking of what we can speak of
In the morning's petulant light
This is, we both know, all we have
This space of distance between now
And when, giving up, you will
Give up your last and weakest breath

When your soul, the energetic
Vitality that is you will
Gently or suddenly be gone
Exhalation in the winter
Between that time and this moment
We have these small conversations
In which we retell the stories
We love and earnestly would keep

Going Though the Cold

The morning was brutal, bone-cold and wet
I closed my jacket, shrank into my scarf
And stepped bravely onto the veranda
Where all was pixelled gray and ashen
My frosted garden, its brittle branches
Eyes tearing, nose running, I looked at it
And thought, "No useful work can come through this,"
Yet work I did for I'd made promises
And so, head bowed, I pushed again forward
Eking out a narrow course in inches
That in retrospect would seem envisioned
A path that stifled pain and cut through cold
And in trudging, stolid, stilted steps
Made an unwitting fool of reticence
And put atop an aerie loft of craft
The speckled doppelganger of foresight

Four Little Pieces

1. Zero to Fifty

My first fifty years
I worked to enlarge myself
Thinking stupidly
That I could deny my death
How beautiful I was then

2. Fifty Till Then

In these second years
I am reducing my size
Knowing as I do
How small a hole death gives us
To pass through without screaming

3. The Universal Beat

In the heart's design
Is life's enduring pattern
First a contraction
Then a graceful letting go
In pulses and beats we live

4. Inheritance

From my father's heart
I learned to exhale slowly
From my mother's mouth
I learned how to inhale rage
How can I deny my birth?

Why Children Should Read Poetry
(for Linda Pastan)

To find that someone else at twelve years old
Had read *The Highwayman* like you had then
And learned to love it – word by precious word
Counting its meters in her blood's rhythm
And in the echoes of her "breathless heart"
Who found in Bess, the landlord's daughter,
The black-eyed image of her mild-eyed mom
And so the bundled world of her childhood
Unraveled with every reading into
An imagined place she could in thinking
Enter, taking out the patterned phrases
Like keys that would open up a future

For me – a chance to clatter and to clash
Over cobblestones to reach my true love
Whose red lips and dark-eyed beauty held me
Whose long black hair flowered in crimson bows
While the copper moon hovers above me
A ghostly ship tossed upon cloudy seas
And the road was a ribbon of moonlight
Oh – it had everything I could want then
The gold, the chase, the chance for love and death

Our Amazing Cactus

There it is outside the wine shed
Rising proud above the awning
Twelve feet tall and still growing strong
Spiny, thick and topped in green shoots
For thirty years it's been with us
First, a prickly, fragile sprout
Among a cluster of cheap plants
Sitting on our first window sill
For weeks it struggled to survive
And was ignored and barely grew
But struggled on as if it knew
That some day we would see it
In a big pot in some new place
Looking lovely like it does now
Reminding us of time's green possibilities
And recognize with proper awe
That something so forlorn and loved
Was living with us all along
While we were busy with our lives

At Night in Cherry Creek

He walked beside me shivering
I was warm in my new wool
He was jittery and wounded
I was calm, my stomach was full
He complained about his mother
I sang the praises of my wife
His journey was just beginning
I was at the end of my life

Triplets 1: Feeling Is First

Feeling is first, he said, and he was right
Before the mind can justify the buy
The heart must be inflamed with aspiration

Feeling is true, he said, it brings in light
When prudent thoughts cast a shadow on choice
The heart points a laser beam at desire

Feeling is hope, he said, when it takes flight
A thousand earthbound wings extend outward
And every imperfect thing reaches for light

Triplets 2: A Lifetime of Our Love

Dinner last night was a lifetime of love
Compressed into sixty minutes of time
First the zeal, then the harm, then the mending

When we sat down your eyes were candlelight
Lit again by some new discovery
Burnt more than once, I followed cautiously

There I was with you in your restaurant
And it was brimming with decent people
I did my best to fit in

Lifted by the lightness of the good will
You drew me safely into your keeping
Throwing out a line I could get hold of

I was happy to have it and held it
Except for one moment – I jerked away
And unwittingly broke the thread you offered

Then the old pantomime began again
Hands climbing up a wall of pettiness
Legs descending a staircase of despair

And then the long, practiced show of silence
Those public seconds that stretch out like claws
The familiar expectancy of loss
Then, fumbling through my tackle box, I found
My own spool of thread wrapped in newspaper
A line of words that went to bridge the gap

And gave us just the finest string of love
To shimmy out on, wiggling as we went
Till finally, we met in the middle

Just then the music started up again
The crowd, put briefly on pause, roared again
And in the happy din we were in love

Triplets 3: Whose Arms?

Whose hands have your hands touched?
Whose lips has your mouth kissed?
What stories can you tell!

What baubles have I given?
What bold promises made?
What history is here!

Here we are together
So many years apart
Let's say and do nothing

There's no past in my heart
No record in my brain
I am filled up with you

At the Green Owl

Look at these three pony-tailed girls
Sipping coffee, talking in rounds
Glittering in the morning sun
Note the man in the wheelchair
Denim jacket and dark tattoos
Ogle Sherrie with her new boobs
Hot pants and saucy attitude
Gaze around at all the artwork
The color-by-number paintings
Plastic owls hooting from the shelves
Smell the coffee grounds, bacon grease
And Sherrie's perfume whipping by

This is how we start our Mondays
Here in Delray Beach, Florida
City of the Green Owl cafe
Pulsing heart of America

Around the counter you will see
Pot-bellied salesmen in short sleeves
Wiry electricians on speed
House painters in white coveralls
Some millionaire eating fried eggs
Charlie, Red, and Bruce, playing cards
Jose, ex-champion and gardener
Big ladies from the Baptist church

This is where I come each morning
Read the paper and write a bit
Remembering how for ten years
Kieran and I met here to talk

Andy, Walking Away

I watched you sauntering away, old friend
Down Atlantic Avenue toward the beach
Walking with that Chaplin canter
Your toes turned out, the lateral tilting
The expectant, modest optimism
That was always your style, even back then
I sometimes made fun of your odd ways then
When we were young and I was so cocksure
But now I can see that it fits you well
And lets me love you more easily now
And regret whatever meanness of mind
My past caring for you carried with it

Four Thirty in the Morning

He wakes, checks the clock – four thirty
He will not sleep again, he knows
He walks to the window, looks out
Upon the lawn and sees her bike
Overturned – it brakes his heart

He won't be there for her first date
Or graduation or wedding
No grandchildren atop his knee
All those Hallmark moments – fuck that
He thinks, fuck everything

The old pain is coming back now
It will wreck his head and make him vomit
He shuts the blinds, shuffles to the bathroom
Downs the pills, takes the hot shower
If he's lucky it will subside

Back to his dark bedroom he walks
And watches his wife – she's snoring
And that too fills him with regret
So he stands there stupidly
Remembering how her mouth looked
When he first bent close to kiss it

How War Has Changed

In my father's time, boys went eagerly
Endured what they were obliged to suffer
Gave gallantly what was taken from them
Became men in the company of men

Nowadays, boys and girls go off eagerly
Enduring what, in hindsight, wasn't needed
Failing to mature and find some comfort
Sacrificing more and taking home less

Then, they gamely returned to grateful towns
Where storekeepers came out to welcome them
Where young women, grown up by loss and toil,
Took their men back in sweet enclosures

Nowadays, shattered, they shuffle homeward
Broken into bits and scarred and tortured
Slipping, unwanted and ignored, alone
Misplaced children in a war-weary world

Old Hem in Idaho

He chose death right – when nothing was left but
The long, bad pain and his strength depleted
He gave up right – when the fight was beaten
When even the good lines were deleted

He was not the same man in those late years
Who had sauntered bull-like into Paris
Undoubting, undaunted, unstopped by fears
Ready to take it all on and fully

First Time Training

The immense separation
The fake-hearty greeting
The cautious stretching out
The sizing up in sidelong glances
The invented conversation
Almost listening to what he says
Almost meaning what you say
And then the moment arriving
Moving to the center of the mat
The resumption of familiar postures
And with a quick touch of hands
The relief that comes from action
Moving into your practiced game
Discovering what you have
Submitting to the natural rhythm
The deconstruction of ego
The liberation of consciousness
Enjoying the gentle sport
Becoming almost a singularity

Trying to Love a Bullfight

It's not the death that really upsets you
Death is, after all, a practical whore
It is not the midday sun that scorches you
That is what all the wide-brimmed hats are for
It is not the cold, stone bench that hurts you
Cheap cushions can be purchased by the door
It's the ritual death in small degrees
That brings you down, with the bull, to your knees

Aunt Rosie's Stories

They begin in the middle, as they should
Then move through the streets of her memory
Slowly, observantly and joyfully
Stopping here and there to point something out
The felicity of a shop window
A slogan on the side of a trolley
The tailoring of a businessman's suit
And then they move on again languidly
To some amusement park or concert hall
Where a young woman with radiant eyes
And black hair and a heart beating for life
Plays out her time of glad expectations
A bright star surrounded by lesser stars
Made darker by her youthful potential
Everything then was ripe with potential
All the streets were glittering and golden
The sky powder blue, the mountains snowy white
The horizon an endless reach of time
Back then when Rosie was young and fetching

Waiting for His Wife to Dress

He strutted back and forth
And yelled up the staircase
"Can't you please hurry up?
We'll be late at this pace!"

But it did him no good
All his constant nagging
"Go alone if you want to,"
She groaned, spirit sagging

De La Rochefoucauld, he read,
Spent such waits writing sayings
Which ensured his renown
And stopped his wife's braying

So he promised himself
He'd wait writing verses
Which improved his humor
And ended the curses

A Year After the Marriage

They stood on the shore facing the ocean
Listening to the surf break, the culling birds
The waves lifted themselves up like lions
Then rushed toward them, a shimmering stampede
In the distance they could see green hills
Retreating discreetly from the shoreline
Behind them a ragged ridge of mountain
A year ago they were married here
On this very beach on a brighter day
She remembered her dress and the candles
He could still recall the taste of Champagne
A cool wind stirred, he reached out for her hand
But she was gone already, he knew that

Cold Morning in June

Cold morning in June
What did I say to cause it?
The bed sheets are cold
I will not touch them again

Tourist Tips for Jaipur

Hire an experienced driver
And then trust your fate to his skill
Don't fret the frenzied highways
The blaring buses, honking cars
Megalomaniacal motorbikes
Lumbering oxcarts, lazy cows
Clattering people-stuffed rickshaws
Dutiful camels, impudent pigs
And supercilious monkeys
Ignore even the elephants
That amble against the current
Coming home after a day's work
They are all there for a reason
Mind your own raison d'être
And let the wayward driver drive

The Ur God Opens His Eyes

I

Into some timeless, thoughtless, lightless, wordless abyss
A fragrant thought opened up, lotus-like,
   in the mind of the god
A two-petaled emanation containing all pain and bliss
Joining light to dark, ambition to renunciation
Tenderness to heartlessness and wealth to desolation

II

It was a change of mood, Tagore imagined, that set free
A frozen, four-faced Brahma from his immobile stance
Who breathed into every valley, plain and mountain
The seed of vitality that broke open the shell of promise
Setting into motion the ineluctable swell of life

III

And from those early living forms there grew
The pull and tug of lifting up and settling down
The replications and the evolutions
Agriculture, commerce, art and meditation
And every thought and feeling that was born from that

IV

And so it was in that stark and wordless void
Roaring unchecked across the primordial ether
Refulgent as a thousand burning asteroids
The first eternal and expanding ohm
Animating every dead thing into life

V

And in that first eruption every form was divided
From what-would-have-been to what-will-always-be
And so something old was also something new
And even love was fractured and with it every
    uttered sigh
That old lovers say to one another just before they die

Outside of Udaipur

Outside of Udaipur there is marsh
That holds the remnants of old Hindu shrines
Beside it on a rise one temple stands
Above the rest and seemingly untouched
Cut from golden marble slabs into vaults
Whose every surface displays gods and kings
Warriors and lovers, bulls and monkeys
An overwhelming monument to art
Which like the great basilica in Rome
Humbles and provokes those who now pass through
Wonder for what skillful hands once made these
Thousands of manufactured images
Whose hands and feet were so carefully shaped
It's nearly perfect – except every face
Is damaged in some way: flattened, bludgeoned
By invaders whose god commanded them
To hide their women in headscarves and screens
To murder or enslave unbelievers
And deface the image of human life

In Old Delhi

Through the dark streets of Old Delhi
Traffic streams in one direction
Rickshaws, bikes and pedestrians
Battle one another for some advantage
And then fall back into the channel
On either side merchants sit and wait
Or haggle boisterously with passing shoppers
Fighting for some fleeting lift in cash flow
That time will flatten out before day's end

In fits and starts our barefoot driver
Pulls us through the frenzied loop
Passing gilded saris brightly spun
Bronze pots and bins of spice and cigarettes
Just as it was a hundred years ago
But for the cluster of connecting wire
That runs above us all along the way

End of Day

No need to go outside to feel the evening's glow
Or walk the woods to know the trees are going dark
When brooding dusk refutes the rosy hue of daytime
And renders dull the detail that was clean and stark

No need to leave the house to know the ink is dimming
That in the day delineated every blade
We know the sun-lit world although drawn in brightness
Will leave no trace of what was etched when
    daytime fades

We have said goodbye to countless daytimes
And sat in wonder through a thousand nights
Yet always awakened to morning's kindness
And started out again with fresh delight

But this time I can feel the darkness that is coming
Will not renew itself in yet another gleaming dawn
And so tonight I will remain here in our bedroom
And hold you close until the light of day is gone

The Best Gift

Her best gift to me
Was for too long ungiven
She spent her last breath
On the purchase of my heart
And left me counting backwards

How They Talked

He wants to know how
She wants to know when and why
He tells her I will
She misconstrues his syntax
Such is the grammar of love

Lost Sunday

It began early in the morning
Before the sun lit up our room
Onto the cold wood I put my feet
And stood and left our bed
And showered and dressed
An hour later up in my studio
Sitting at my desk, sipping coffee
I could do nothing but stare out
Onto the still-darkened street below
Waiting for something to come
But nothing did
It was in the way she said goodnight
That perfunctory tone, so familiar
Yet so empty of affection
That made the thoughts go dry
It was after so long gone now
Before she stirred I was sure

The Artist's Nudes

They changed over time
The master's ladies
Round then soft
Then sharp, then lost

Oh, those early girls!
Those ripe and ready girls
What fun to be a maestro then
To paint and fuck and paint again!

Then came the ephemeral stage
The wispy, effervescent things
How tough it was to light their day
How easily they slipped away

And later at his life's long end
Those woeful, weary women
How well they played their part
How little did they care for art

America Speaking

1. The Immigrant

The immigrant loves me
Waiting by the side of the road
Watching for a truck to slow
Hablando con sus amigos
He is happy to have come this far
To have worked so hard and saved so long
And paid the many *propinas* that must be paid
He remembers kissing his wife goodbye
Holding his *niña* tenderly, making promises
The long, dusty, claustrophobic ride
And the first view of his new country
The overwhelming hope
He is here now, here, waiting
If he gets work today
He'll make ten dollars an hour
As much as he made in two days in Peru
Don't tell me, he thinks, I am not welcome
Don't tell me I do not deserve this chance
Don't tell me there is no work for me
I am here and I can see: America needs me

2. The Firefighter

The firefighter loves me
Lying on the station's couch
Thumbing through an old magazine
Watching a rerun of *Law and Order*
He is happy to know I chose him

Proud to be one of my children
And although his body is resting now
It is ready. His back is strong
His legs sturdy, his grip firm
He is waiting for the alarm to ring
And when it does he will be the first
The first to the truck
The first to the blaze
The first to glory
That is how much he loves me

3. The Farmer

The farmer loves me
Sitting on his front porch
Looking out at his land
Three hundred acres, all arable
The crops harvested now
The fields lying fallow
Everything is good now
In the old days it was thus
At this late, quiet time of the year
And then there was the drought
And now the market has returned
He smokes his hickory pipe
And thinks about his children
All busy in different cities
Bunched up with buildings
Noisy, crowded places
Glass and steel and the ever-present
Haste that entangles millions
What strength it takes to live like that

Yet he is proud of them
And happy to have this space and time
After the harvest is done

4. The College Teacher

The college teacher loves me
Sitting alone in her classroom
After her students have departed
She thinks about her own best teacher
Who hugged a fourteen-year-old girl
And wiped away each reluctant fear
And came in early Monday mornings
To tutor her privately in English
"This is our secret," she said
"Nobody has to know."
And patiently, in a year's time,
Erased the ugly accidents of her birth
And brought her into fluency
Which made it possible in small degrees
To merge into the beautiful ignorance of things
And show up, several years later, at the top
Most accomplished, best dressed, most loved
And finally, after college, best married
With luck and love and money
And for all that and more how happy she is
To be back here looking for herself

5. The Car Washer

The car washer loves me
Rag in hand, ready to pounce

When each clean car emerges
Glistening, dripping and happy
From the amazing machine
He is there to rub them down
These shiny steel, four-wheeled
Pets of the wealthy class
To each pampered beast
He moves with alacrity and zest
There is no room in his heart
Nor time in his workday
To hate the owners or his
Pot-bellied, cigar chomping boss
He has other jobs to do, other burdens
And these hulking creatures
Wet and happy from their shower
Do not deserve to be badly handled
They are pretty, mindless things
And one day, not now but one day
He will have one of his own

6. The Copywriter

The copywriter loves me
When the results are published
And he sees the response rate for Split B
The six-tenths of one percent lift
He is deeply happy. He has become richer
By eleven thousand dollars and what is more
He has proven his point
If battle victories were as sweet
He might be a soldier
But marketing is love, not war

And his words are silky feathers
His sentences healing balms
Restoring youth and hope to the millions
He has no cudgels to swing
Just metaphors like bubbles
That swell up and disappear
He is a lover, not a fighter
And he tells himself that every day
In the morning, washing his face
In the mirror's bright reflection

7. The Real Estate Developer

The real estate developer loves me
Hard-hat on her sixty-dollar haircut
Master plan under her scented armpit
Cashmere socks coddling her legs
Standing before her towering condominium
Head back, she is quietly amazed at its size
Its capacity to absorb interest
Its potential to yield profit
It was always a labor of love
She lives in a modest house alone
Sees her children on weekends
And reads biographies of great men
Particularly Einstein and Napoleon
Audacity! That was their secret
That's what she says at parties

8. The Bartender

The bartender loves me
Rag in his back pocket
Bad pants, good shoes
He moves beautifully
Like a young cat on a counter
His braceleted arms are graceful
His ringed hands are adept
He has mastered the arts
The complex art of smiling
The subtle art of the hands
The thoughtful, accidental touch
Lingering but just a second
Every night is an opportunity
To be beautiful and smooth
And bend easily toward love
For if he knows one thing
He knows he is there for love

After Eighty Years

Fifty years I worked
To solidify myself
Thirty more I tried
To become ephemeral
Each seemed a fitting purpose

But now that I'm here
Inside this winter garden
I see my true form
The rhythm everything shares
Constriction and relaxing

Dreaming of Tigers

After school I cannot linger
With the other girls but hurry
To help my widowed father work
At the family restaurant

Customers come and eat and go
My father works hard to please them
I keep my head down when I work
And move among them like a ghost

After work he watches TV
I sit in the kitchen reading
We don't talk about silly things
Mother approved of silly things

When I dream we are together
On the stoop in the moonlit night
Above us up on the street lamps
White tigers are walking, watching

How to Defend Your Clients in Newark

This is how you defend your clients,
    Mr. Bergrin explained
You work hard. You stay up late. You answer
    their phone calls,
Explain the law to them, look for loopholes
But the best defense against a charge of murder
Is to discredit or eliminate the witness
I do my job. I'd do anything for my clients

The witness was named Deshawn McCray
The people on the street called him Kimo
No Kimo, Bergrin told his clients, No case
Three months later the case was dropped

In front of a shuttered bar and grill
On 18th Street and S. Orange
Kimo stood with his girlfriend
He seemed relaxed, a witness said
He was laughing

Above the side door, she noticed
An air conditioner leaning down
Like an old lady, watching the neighborhood decline

After Dinner There Was the Long Drive Home

After dinner there was the long drive home
He was bone tired and his head was foggy
Anxious to get into his bed and sleep
She, in contrast, was flushed with the evening
Brimming with all the new information
Eager to examine the choice pieces

This was always a fragile time for them
After the drinking and conversation
Something delicate always unraveled
Some partly uttered thought or grim notion
Or ebb in the flow of conversation
That broke the thin ice of their alliance

He eased the car into the passing lane
She said she didn't like the maitre d'
He thought, "This fucking guy won't let me in."
"Same old fucking MO, I see," she said.
He gripped the wheel, turned to her and said, "What?"

They drove the rest of the way home in silence

He parked the car. She got out, went inside
He stopped at the bottom of the staircase
Listened to the clacking of her footsteps
And it nearly broke his heart to listen
Later, in the den, watching the boob tube
He imagined that they were just lovers
She took her time, showered and brushed her hair
Put on her nightgown and lay down reading

She read the same chapter three times over
Thinking, "I will not do this anymore."
She turned off the light and welcomed the dark
And shut her eyes, still moist, and fell asleep

While they were sleeping, two spirits rose up
One tiptoed upstairs, the other downward
And met together halfway in between
Embraced and, as evanescent things do,
Became a single unsubstantial thing
That had no form or mass or resistance

In Front of the Cathedral

Sun on a stone old wall
You, seated, reading the guidebook
Brahms, an open door
I am counting the churches
So much and yet not enough

At the Hotel Piazza in Johannesburg

You can't smoke inside, the bartender says
But on the second floor there is a place
A patio where you can sit and smoke

A table, two chairs, an ashtray and this
Broad view of the country to the mountains
This city is so far from everything

Back to front, the columbine ridge
Coming forward, dark green hills, then the roofs
Of the old townships, brown and black and gray

Then a meridian of parks and ponds
Then townhouses painted in sienna
For the country's new rich such as they are

A hedgerow of cypress, a redbrick wall
A swath of green grass before the entrance
Then the date palms and white bougainvillea

Till finally, this – this hideout with a view
A pigeon alights on the balustrade
Blinking, he waits for me to feed him

Breakfast at the Casino

The sky was painted
The piazza was a prop
Yet in her retiring smile
He saw lush green refuge
Where they could live

Inside the Taxi

She had dressed herself like a Chinese fairy doll
Sparkling details, brightly draped in primary colors
There was a careful carelessness about the arrangement
As if to pretend she understood what she was doing
Her fingernails, for example, had been painted gold
But that was weeks ago – there was a gap of color now
She said she was a champion at tae kwon do
And spoke confidently and smiled when she wanted
She was everything, in short, that he was not but wanted
When they shook hands goodbye she had an easy grip
So when she promised to send him photos,
    he did not believe her

In LA: Calling You on a Whim

After sixty hours of planes and taxis
And little speeches and difficult conversations
A life I have lived since before you were born
I was here in LA, bound for Baltimore
With 30 hours till my next appointment
And so, when I called you, I expected nothing
But there you were, happy to hear from me
Glad I was in town, eager to meet for dinner
You will not know how good a moment that was
Until you have a full grown child of your own
And decide to interrupt him, busy working on
   his new career
Until, before hitting send, your mind races through
All the little ways you might have failed him

How My Father Dressed

When my father was twenty-one
He dressed in starched cotton shirts
And pressed linen suits and silk ties
And bore the wide smile
Of a confident man

When my father was forty-one
He wore gabardine tweed jackets
And flannel shirts and thin knit ties
With the casual elegance
In the manner of his calling

When my father was sixty-one
He put his fine shirts and ties away
And wore cotton slacks and sweaters
Displaying the happy nonchalance
Of a new grandfather

When my father was eighty-one
He dressed like a blind man
In soup stained shirts and mismatched socks
Exhibiting the sad but wise look
Of a man who had stopped caring

An Irish Love Story

At a different time in a different place
Before we first came face to face
There stood a castle by the Sea
Of Donegal called Erin Lea

In that mighty fortress stayed
A princess whose rare beauty made
Each suitor turn from flesh to stone
When first her smile to him was shown

So great was this effect on men
She was not irked or angry when
Her father chose as her fair groom
A blind man out of Brigadoon

And so it was when I met you
My body hardened through and through
Yet with my eyes I could convey
How happily beat my heart that day

My heartfelt message was received
And by your answer was relieved
To know that I would be your man
And thus began our life's sweet span

The Last Defense of Carlos Perez-Olio

He came in stooped over and wailing in pain
There was gunshot in his belly and rum in his brain
His wound was superficial but his pain was deep
My wife is in the car. I think she fell asleep
But when we saw her our hearts filled with dread
For there was blood all over her head
She was, we guessed, shot by the same gun
That shot her husband Carlos but instead of one
Fired bullet she had three in her noggin
At least that was what the nurses logged in
They forced us off the road, he remembered later
I loved that woman, no one hated her
There were three of them in a yellow Camry
They wore baseball caps so I couldn't see
Them well, but one had a mustache, that I recall
His eyes were dark. His hands were small
He wanted our money. He threatened to shoot
We gave him everything and our rings to boot
But that was not enough for him
He made a joke and on a whim
He shot my wife three times I'm sure
And aimed at me with hatred pure
And shot me once and quick I fell
Into the dark then ran like hell
And though he shot three times more
He did not hit me. He did not score.
Weeks later deep in Echo Lake was found
An unmarked handgun in the muddy ground
That was all there was to take
Till three months after Peggy's somber wake

Carlos claimed a policy on her sacred life
$467,000 was the payoff for his wife
Carlos himself was a criminal attorney
Who'd defended 30 murderers but set none free
Yet he was surprised when his legal claim
Was turned down though his legal name
Was clearly indicated as the sole beneficiary
But you are a suspect, the police told him.
You are not free.
And three months later he was put in the pen
By twelve brave and honest men
Who hated crime and wanted to show
Carlos Perez-Olio
That defending murder is a better way
To live than murdering for the pay

My Grandfather's Morning Tea

It was a steep walk up
From his thatched roof home
To get to where the peat was
Up on the top of his two acres
He climbed it every morning
And twice when guests were coming
And all before his first cup of tea
After breakfast he worked the land
From the cottage to the weir
He worked all day at that
And then, at dusk, stood by the lea
Looking out and dreaming

Here We Go Again

Here we go rumbling down the buckled road
Past the still ranches and deserted farms
Where happy boys, on horseback, herded cows
Easy in their saddles along the fields
Lush with summer corn or wheat or sorghum

Here we go paddling along the river
Speckled whiteness and dark patches of green
Where brown bodied trout slithered and bounded
Shimmering and bright in the sparkling light
Of the first sunlit promise of the day

Here we go rattling along the steel rail
Past empty buildings and the old depot
On which men once stood, looking down the tracks
Waiting for their hectic days to unfold
Hoping for fortune to emend their lives

Here we go clapping along the boardwalk
Past the wind-blown, salt-bleached, clean-swept
    shoreline
Where once children splashed gaily in the waves
And played boisterously in the white sand
As if to awake a slumbering world

Here we go marching through the city night
Past steel and glass cathedrals of false hope
Designed by fools we labeled geniuses
For an innocent generation that
Knew everything was good and would endure

Here we go tiptoeing through the graveyard
Past the crumbling headstones of our parents
Whose own travels are all but forgotten
Except for the stories we carry with us
Bound tightly around the parchment of love